EQUIPOISE

EQUIPOISE

— POEMS —
Kathleen Halme

Sarabande Books
LOUISVILLE, KENTUCKY

Managing Editor
Sarabande Books, Inc.
2234 Dundee Road, Suite 200
Louisville, KY 40205

LIBRARY OF CONGRESS CATALOGING-IN-PUBLICATION DATA

Halme, Kathleen.
    Equipoise / Kathleen Halme.
        p.   cm.
    ISBN 1-889330-19-1 (cloth: alk. paper). — ISBN 1-889330-20-5
    (pbk.: alk. paper)
    I. Title.
PS3558.A3955E69 1998
811'.54—dc21   98-4805
                                                          CIP

Cover painting: "Fathom" by Marilyn Greenberg. Used by kind
permission of the artist.

Cover and text design by Charles Casey Martin.

Manufactured in the United States of America.
This book is printed on acid-free paper.

Sarabande Books is a nonprofit literary organization.

Grateful thanks to Dick and Nancy Graham, Al Lyons, Anne Axton,
and Anonymous for their generous support of Sarabande Books.

For Alan

On my volcano grows the Grass
A meditative spot—

Emily Dickinson, #1677

· ONE ·

We Grow Accustomed to the Dark

No one
would know of this.

Two boys idling
an aqua speedboat
did not say no
to the simple question from the dock;

we stepped off,
and shot down
the black sash of river

past the tourist battleship
and the alligator circus,
past the raw bar's open
ears of oysters,
past the ladyghost in the library,
past five high church spires,
past the cotton shop
where we bought summer
floating on our bodies,
past her street, Orange, and
past my street, Ann,
past the live oaks dangling Spanish moss,
past the girl under the live oaks
now relieved of the burden of her virginity,
past the stone wall's fondled holes for cannons,
past the square where slaves in chains were sold,
past the peanut stand and beaded pigeons,
past the scrapyard's parts
of redbrown merchant ships,
past the swampside's hulls of wooden boats,

past the fresh babies, and sound sleepers,
the glubbing clay pipes of plumbing,
and cloth-covered wiring,
past the slack lights
of all the last houses,

down the black sash of river,
back down, all the way to ocean.

Where the Cape Fear Empties into Ocean

In last week's big weather the ocean ate
the gazebo at the fat beach.
Sunday again, they're back:
the fast-food families, staking
claims in swimsuits big as sails.

Plant that cooler of salt snacks and fizz.
Stick that watermelon umbrella
on your little edge of ocean. In the shifting
continental drift of cellulose
we all want the primal dip.

Already a boy has found a baby shark.
He walks it like a clarinet, its jaw
a squeaking reed. The little primate
sneaks behind beached sleepers,
and plays the shark at their butts.

It's too soon to make a fuss:
we're a bit crabby this morning.
I grow nails and teeth,
unroll below the sea oats, and run
with my real husband into ocean.

Can you still touch? Yes, can you?
we ask until everyone in water
has dissolved below the shoulders.
Above us all, a whalish blimp chubs by
to tell us where to eat tonight.

Below us all,
the bottom dips

down in drift and
we're afloat with
plankton in the neap tide.

Bolted into hunger
we can't fight,
the current floats
us soaked with water.
We can't see

the larval mollusks,
the small sea cucumbers,
invisible to the naked
eye, drifting in
our extraneous suits.

We are in the soup, singular
and swimming, roiling
with the isopods and copepods.
We are motile, every one
of us buoyant

as bubbles
in the tidal cycle. Who can see
our feet kicking
over a great heart
cockle pumping water

into gills, over bulging
ark shells straining

plankton? We are delicious,
surrendered to shells and jellies,
every one soaking in sun.

Lilies Showering Down

I

On that island, I was learning what I loved:
a little life for an animal with eggs.
Clean as a peppermint, I gave off light!

I was slow as soap, my simplicity astounding.
Consider how infinite I was,
walking every inch of that orchid-shaped island:

no jangled thoughts, I knew only elegances:
a storm's wash pinks the beach with jellyfish;
in the salt marsh, visible in water,

a seahorse, small as a baby's finger,
wraps its tail around a reed to stay in place,
or possibly, for pleasure.

II

From way out in the ocean, he came
like a rower, pulling himself in wood
all the way to me.

He loved salt: three-hundred-year-
old meat, the block, the fingertip.
My lips were salt air sea.

I thought: hummingbird.
Miraculous verb, one could be
drawn to land on his salted palm.

Am I at all mysterious to you? he asked.
The blue notion fumed
until it flickered open utterly.

He gave and gave,
then led me close to trumpets
thread on devil's green;

I went under as the open sun
vined up the old snake shack
high at the rim of the sea.

III

Below the fathers drape their mended nets to dry,
the mothers hang bleached
white by white and blue by blue.

I eat provisions I've collected for confinement:
jewel box of fish, a fist of soda bread,
some licorice pipes—black and undeniable.

I sleep alone on the circumference.
These lighthouse walls are five feet thick.
In hurricanes, a town could hide inside,
but this storm abides with me.

Island Incarnation

I have seen a king snake whip and twist itself around
a longer rattlesnake, and when the other's
gorgeous hiss and length went limp,
as the moment spread itself out holy,
and the sea grass bristled a scraping lisp,
I have seen the king make straight
the long black wand of rattler and take her in headfirst:
a gradual assumption of saintly concentration,
until I have seen the very tip, the crenellated rattle
—black cowrie tossed back into the only ocean—
disappear inside the waves of snake.

Grace

The black fish undressed easily on their blue plates.
Smug in love, they went ahead and ordered
chocolate layer cake to celebrate the Red.

Outside the picture window, February blew and bounced
the sun across a beach. Saint Valentine.
She thought about the things she'd like to buy.

Below, three boys in black wet suits were stretching in new skins.
They looped and tossed each other closer to the surf; two coupled
while the other watched, then they recoupled and were watched.

What is there to fear in men? All seed and sullen play, she thought.
And then she saw a crowd of dolphins loop and toss,
fins circling like saws through the sea of possible thought.

Next, there was a moment, not much farther out into the ocean,
when she saw the sea do something strange.
Not much farther out, where water came to water,

she saw the waves turn over and open an old caesura in the sea.
On the meniscus of the moment she was alive in,
a black cut fissured into form.

Is anyone here not innocent? she asked herself, and glasses tinked,
cloth folded, and a fish left its skeleton on a blue plate,
as the slipknot pulled again around the ache of paradise.

Betwixt the Flames and Waves

A line of brown pelicans
like folding chairs
flew above
their love corpuscular.
        The couple looked awkward
        and contemporary,
        as if sex were in it
        and they were scared.

On the undeveloped beach
they sidestepped jellyfish,
clear and small
as babies' brains.
        Shell scrack, shellfish,
        mermaid's purse:
        everything said big.
        Soon they would come to touch.

Another moment and
they would
turn to one and other.
Around their feet,
        under ocean, water
        licked ten thousand
        reps of fleurs-de-lys,
        in an old design.

The couple felt
ridiculous and clean.
Waves slapped a ring
between them in the sand.

No one made a move.
How had it happened
that they had lost
the motions?

· TWO ·

Going to Sea

New at this, we run a freighter aground
and crash a ferry into a merchant ship
before we get control.
Then we're both captain,
laughing with the landscape
flowing past us, strangers in a simulation room,
steering every kind of ocean.

Past ports and docks and iron cranes,
we bang around the loaded dark.
He masters the controls and sets a course. Without me.
As we rush Hamburg and Leningrad,
I shift the view belowdecks, hoping to see
people sliding sideways with their bar snacks—
crustaceans in cracked shells—
blond hair falling away from blond shoulders,
knuckles smudging polished brass,
subtle Scandinavian flirtation,
as they shift in the drift of our play.

I try again and he gives me a woolly look.
"I want to see other people," I say.
"We are the other people," he says, pressing
the anchor icon on the screen,
as we come to on the open sea.

Knots

Is that young couple ahead of us
on their honeymoon? I ask. *Don't stare,*
my polite Southern husband suggests. But they look
so small and wounded leaning on their car.
How worried he seems; she's pinched and disappointed
as though she'd like to fly away in white.
Like us, they probably got the call in bed.

The whiskery men parked behind us
are as coupled as a coquina.
They're hauling a fishing boat of beer back to land.
The tall one asks outright: *This your honeymoon?*
The girl wipes *yes* onto her boy-husband's chest.
Already they have been wounded by weather they didn't ask for.
Elegant, the smaller man hands them a cantaloupe
bigger than a human head.
Maybe you could break it on that rock, he says.

She reaches in the car to find the knife,
ribboned in small lilies and satin streamers.
Silver glints in the sun's Latin
as she holds the full moon on her palm
and cuts. The four eat until they are familiar.
When juice drips down her seashell feet,
she laughs, and her partner visibly
breathes again in each divisible cell.

At last the ferry huffs into our view. We fit inside
our vehicle and drive aboard. We're on water now,
pulling safely shore to shore; behind us
the white lighthouse still binds us to the island.
Is *that* the land we're going to—

the mainland clouded in its own communion?
We pass over slowly, by glances,
holding to our own love,
alive astride lighthouse and gray scarf of horizon.

Until the Day Breathes and the Shadows Flee

Miniature stone mansions line a sighing town
of death, where snowdrops bell like wedding gowns
of girls given early to shaping dreams
sewed to ivory guilt's forgiving grief.

Eulalia and Grace and Ada are gone.
Their stones keep vows with men who died young.
Reasonable self in death's big company,
one husband's stone still keeps close custody:

I go ahead to make a place for you.
What matters here is perpetuity.
What's buried here in secret interests me.
What vows were given them to keep, what vows

were perfidy? Did he loathe her kneading
bread, then spread his risen slices thick
because he could? Did she keep one bed?
When he found her heat and quelled the lace,

what did they call the violet miracle
that their antebellum bodies made?
I'll try to ask this more elegantly:
what will last the ocean of a life—

the words, a lover, compassion's craft?
Hold back the beaming white spirea—
all overclothed glances evaporate,
an unlaced evanescence.

Until the day breathes and the shadows flee,
everyone here in sighing town will sleep

in the moon as the moon wears down
forgivable half-souls swallowed whole.

Flowers of the South

Tell me Lula's strange—I'll disagree.
Neighbors talk about her door: it's purple.
They think it hides some Old World mystery.
Ivy knits a net around her house, warps
the clapboard and binds the orbit
of the whale weather vane: a gift to women
left widowed by a captain's bad order.
She places tartlets on a doilied plate, then
unwraps photos of the last disaster:
the smashed portico they tried to fix
on her stucco house in Parma. I ask her
if she's been back. "No," she says, "I've been sick."
Her mantel clock chimes four. Its gold dolphin
pulls a sea nymph out into the open.

Plain Poem

God help me. I get full beauty
in moments, in flashes. Take yesterday,
a true spring, Easter egg morning:

I see him at dawn on the porch next door,
folded on our neighbor's red rocker,
head tucked like a mourning dove, sleeping

a slumped down, untroubled sleep.
He's right out of 1930s movies I've seen:
brown fedora and brown suit, blue bow tie,

cotton shirt starched to shining.
He's old. He's sleeping. He's black
on a street where some still pray

to keep new buyers of old houses white.
We call our nice neighbor. "He seems fine,"
she says, "whoever he is, he just wants to rest—

says he's waiting for a dark-skinned man.
He doesn't want a ride; he just wants to rest."
We wrap a hot cross bun then go out to check.

He's still sleeping his old gentleman's sleep.
When a soft-spoken police officer stops by,
the man can't recall his name or address.

The young officer gentles him on his arm
to the white patrol car idling at the curb,
and even though the man clearly does not want

to bow his head and get in back,
there is no balking or pushing to be seen
as we turn and go inside to have spring sex.

New Worlds to Buy

Freight train or riverboat horn?
Who cares? Both moan.
It seems we're staying put
in the landscape we'll never get used to:
big palms and a fuss of narcissus
on Christmas—nervy green set up as scenery.

Beyond the porch, the road's as smooth as Sunday pants.
When the Bible Belt lets out another notch,
where's the good guilt,
the woolly fabrication, the hunch
and hope that melts the saints?
As slow as crows, as open water all winter,
we rock, too relaxed to see
between the dog and tree.

Beignets for Breakfast

This town's a squeaking bed,
and every room's been painted red
to hide our rising dread.

All the cuckoo clocks have stopped
and time's let loose like hollyhocks
climbing powder-sugared walks.

This town is lush with hummingbirds
whirring in a larkspur blur
of long reflexive verbs.

Blue orchids work voodoo,
but how can one find breathing room
in such frou-frou overbloom?

I can't hear my own heart think
in this town of swans and stinks
where every standard poodle drinks.

Objects of Desire

Soap, soap, soap.
God's in the letter *O*
and in the rural South, tonight
everyone smells like soap.

This auction house is dirty,
but we're washed clean
and we want more stuff
from the hard altar of objects
riding the luscious earth.

The auctioneer, a famous Southern psychotic,
dips in the mysteries and blesses
the souls of fezzes and figurines.
His milk glass eye sees
every   living   thing   increase.
Jar a marbles
three DOLLAr bill
two dollar sir
two bucks GONE
I almost wanted that.

The second hand started
and the light does work—
with clock now!
Five bucks GONE
Thank you ma'am.
SOLD! and the new-owned object
swelters with intention
in the wet hands of redemption.

This week in Bosnia a girl was raped repeatedly
then traded by the enemy
"for a *major appliance,*" the paper said.
In auction talk that's not specific enough:
Sixty dollar on that refrigerator
that was working when we took it
out of the lady's house.
That's better.
Now we know where we sit
in chance and in contrition.
Round hatbox full of lady's Sunday hats now.
Tempting, but where do we find faith
in this amphibium of stuff and death?
Until last year I owned one plate.
What's more, I've sinned in other ways,
but tonight, as witness to this litany,
my mind's a prayer in pure perfume,
a prayer in pure perfume.

The Subjunctive of Pomegranate

Maybe I could forgive what people cannot help
if I had lived through war.
If it were the same Eve and Adam kissing
in paradise in Persia I would guess
the fruit they shared was one of these
round bombs. They had to work
conditions contrary to facts, force
desire down, thumb on thumb, break up
the ruby fist. A bite would have exploded
had one been taken. Nothing chewable, a globe
to hold in both hands, press down, deeper
down. A ragged wound would forgive the tangled fruit.

While the Sea Laughed Itself into a Foam

When we built that beach house out on the cape,
we never worried, we didn't think at all
that a beach is land given by wind and wave.

Our shingled house was born to this landscape.
On the deck you couldn't see the retaining wall
they'd built for new houses out on the cape.

The day we installed a sun weather vane
it spun around although the sea was calm,
and no one was moved by wind or waves.

We hadn't finished hanging linen drapes,
and family and new friends began to call
to see our progress out on the cape.

One spring storm and we saw our cliff edge stray;
rolls of sod, new myrtles began to fall
and were tossed away by wind and waves.

Soon, the seawall couldn't take the strain
and caved, then our cliff went down in the squall.
When we fled the beach house out on the cape,
we left a table set for wind and waves.

Ocean with Whale

Whale tail, tale of whale:
a black hook poised to pull us in,
a fine nib dipped,
scraper to unpaint the sky—
like good sin, a barnacled
rocket that swims.

"You're coming too close
to shore!" the sea grass groans
in the panic language of grasses.
But she oversees her own
scenery—swirls and eddies
surround her. She made them
and she'll make more.

· THREE ·

Avulsion

And though I grieved, my time in hell
was sure and short. Those gaseous veins
of gorgeous mineral states told me more
than I could know on the sedgy plains of earth.

There was no voice like yours
in hell. The saxophones were verdigris
and cold. There was no voice at all,
not yours, and not my own.

I cannot say whose empty house it was
that burned throughout the wrinkled night.
I can tell you that morning brought intelligent
blue light not seen by anyone on earth.

I don't remember much—just this:
the lid was screwed on tight
and no one cared if heaven fell
to earth or gathered us in light.

Intro to Creative Writing

Sara K. has no pelt, no dermis, no hide.
Sara K.'s a peeled apple trailing a curl of skin.

Those Ceylon sapphires are eyes that stayed open
all night. Sara K. is a buzzword

in the fierce virgin class, the antierotic league.
"Give details, don't be so abstract," they stress.

"What's a 'lot bone stick'?" a surfer/student asks,
glancing at Sara K.'s bobbing woman's breasts.

I ask myself, what's the verb for incest?
as though I could find her

words. Sara K. pulls on her brass locket;
a folding heart conceives a scream.

The Wanton, Harmless Folds of Dreams

"You are an elegant mechanic, a site of tattooed beauty,"
she answers him in the odd erotic present,
ratchet, hex wrench, oilcan, spread below
the rising mountain where they lounge,
plush and gorgeous—clothed!
"My shepherdess, I'm here
because you asked for me.
It's time to use your eggs."
His robe falls open to her water silk.
She glances down and sees
the mystery revised. It's as plain as paper,
written in crisscrossed little zippers,
cursive on his come-true skin.
O body, she prays, how will I ever open?
O body, how will I open him?

Pushing Narcissus

Dear mirror man, here we are: the others.
This hangnail is hers,
that mole over his heart is not about you.
Must we wait until we walk holes through our rag rugs
before you ask us anything about us?
Mirror, skiddle, fall dee dee.
We have heard your sad self's story.

Take your hand out of your pants and drive
to buy a goldfish—
Carassius auratus, native to eastern Asia—
scooped into a plastic bag of water.
Heading home, avoid the bulging mirror.

Now, slip the fish into a filled space of its own.
Give it a fitting name (not your own).
That fish will float unless you feed it.
Watch until you see what gives her pleasure,
watch until she's swimming tangerine.

Autotomy

n. Zool. The spontaneous casting off of a body part, as the tail of certain lizards, for self-protection.

Queen bees of the fait accompli,
I AM
an angel, a princess, a saint and
I am weary of your need
for me to join your coterie.

When the pink and blue cake is cut
again,
don't give me the third degree.
Why must I explain myself to you and you?
I don't ask why
you choose the squeeze and squeal.

Besides,
you wouldn't want me
in your mommy club.
I grew pleasure breasts; these tits
are having a party right in their bra.
Excuse me, Myrmidons of motherhood,
do you love sex?

"Going to Europe again?" you ask,
preening your split ends.
Yes, I am
because I am
a childfree shepherdess.

Between you and me,
how do you like your life?
Do I remind you of what could be?

Who's bitter, dear breeder?
Selfish? Ha!
In twenty years—or so—you'll be home free.

Antidote to Adultery

It is possible that
the starched lot of the couple next door
could let love's genius loose again
and bed down with the corner sun.

If so, would she look up at him
as he noticed her hands
holding something ripe enough to eat
if they gave in again?

One could say they have been
working on saving their marriage,
spreading bought soil that came heavy in bags,
counting on waves and waves of some new plan.

A Study in *O*

Although they felt the chromosomal undertow,
they were prone to follow the old code, and so
no one misspoke.
No one allowed the holy smoke to shroud a throaty episode.
No one moaned an orgy of self-reproach.
The dead bolts on their homes had not corroded.
No one misspoke.

One cold morning on the corner
of Oak and DeSoto, they said hello...
the old vertigo flowed and
overflowed. Even though
they had hoped to postpone
the whole explosion,
no one misspoke.

· FOUR ·

Girls/Metaphor/Meat

He was not the one who had to kill
and kill and kill to get the meat.
His saw cut rib eye, round, and Boston butt;
my father made his living *cutting* meat.

When he was young behind the butcher case,
and handsome in a bishop's paper cap,
he'd slip a cold cut on my finger.
I made it dance ballet as he buzzed

and slapped great slabs of beef.
Home, he grilled state-shaped steaks
and speared them on the plates.
They ate and ate.

In eighth grade my girlfriend
was cooking chicken with her mother,
tugging out the bag of purple parts, when
her own blood began. She came to

and couldn't eat meat again.
We suffered other rites alone:
deviled ham and fox head furs
staring us down at funeral lunches,

rump roast seeping through communion.
"Eat!" they screamed. "You'll get anemic."
We mouthed the quiet hum of vegetables:
I can't eat what I am!

Interstices and Protuberances

Corn segues like greening shades of thought,
prepared to shoot abstraction from the sky,
and girls in pink and violet sweats are taught
to pull the drooping silk and so untie
the creamy ears' alleged concupiscence.
Spilled roots and corn and silk; the boys work near.
One hidden girl stops taking silk. Intense,
she strips the green, each blade, and cups the ear.
Confirmed now, she thumbs the ivory teeth,
and stretching up to meet the torch, she bites,
and tastes her first surprise of milk-white sweet.
This is good, she thinks as she unfolds the rite
and listens for the warming schwa of growing form
she hears inside the rows, the stalks, the corn.

A Dialogue Between the Shepherdesses and Mowers

First was the word as one clay symbol made
and I thought long on shaping worlds I'd rake
below the blue-black waves to row to city's shore,
but love's sleek coating soon wore down on streets
of sharks and skates dressed for the pretty kill:

Shepherdess: Take it someplace else.
Mower: Make us.
Shepherdess: Come here and kick my ass.
Mower: Come here and suck my dick.
Shepherdess: I would if you had one.
Mower: I'll shove that moon right down your throat.
Shepherdess: It's my moon too. Go fuck yourself.

Core

The night desire stood up between me and my friend,
I told him this:

My best friend and I picked green apples
and put them in our undershirts where we'd have breasts.
The apples bumped out as we rode down Suicide Hill.

At the old mine she asked me, "Ever broken a window?"
and smashed one with a rock.
"Now you," she said, and I threw low.
The frosted pane crashed like a waterfall.

Then we could see inside: a lab of sorts,
all white and stainless steel.
On the counter was a fawn, calm and seated,
watching like a little sphinx.

Then he put his finger to my lips.
Then he found my breasts.
It was time in the long unsaid between us.

Through the Dark Sod, as Education

I

Not one strawberry
in those market stalls is bigger than a child's nose
and all are spiced with local sun.
The men sell ponderous smoked fish, gold and redolent,
or they stand on the rim talking with other men.
Full women walk birch baskets home.
As it should be:
the market, and baking, and Saturday bath.

As it should be for me:
strong coffee and apple pastry at an outdoor café
where I am the only one alone.
The morning paper says, "This nation,
despite its people's problems with depression,
will not import the pink happiness pill
so widely prescribed in America."
If we see the sun again today,
imagine our happiness.

An old woman is pushing a sad polka
out of her lifelong accordion
for the newly engaged girl at the next table.
She is clearly a girl, in this country or any.
When her friends kiss her and present her
with a lacy paper cone of salmon roses,
the color of this morning's sprained sun,
she is diaphanous. My mind thinks this
because it is starved for beauty.

Now, a young mother with her baby,
riding a big buggy like a sea captain,
parks near the table of laughing girls, and
gives the baby a biscuit from her bag.
She is waiting for coffee with sugar cubes
wrapped in sketches of famous classical composers.
In this country women wear their babies like corsages.

Across the café, a gypsy fortune-teller's
froth of skirts is motioning to me.
I look down and study the configuration
of crumbs the sparrows will eat when I go home.
In what language would she tell me
her version of myself? Would she say,
"Are you not a lucky one,
you who hear your own mind think?"

      II

Yesterday, I biked through the red, green, blue
countryside, overjoyed at sun;
I rode past a man, about my age,
standing in front of a high woodpile—
ax resting on blond chips—masturbating.

Down the dark string of river woven
into pines below my window,
rain fell and fell into a small wooden boat,
bright blue outside, bright green inside,
pulled to sea behind a tug called *Hope*.

In the language of this country,
what is the word for the tall pine tops,
long at night when the dark outlines
the last light, tall as masts of thought
when we are under god,
in the night that isn't night?

III

Look! A wedding party is assembling
at the yellow wooden church across the street.
I've been inside that unlocked church at night
and seen the intricate miniature sailing ship
hanging low enough for anyone to reach.

The rose girls at the café are suddenly silenced:
it's the bride being eased out of a dark sedan.
When she smoothes out her lily dress,
the girls breathe "Oh!" as one.
May they be happy all day.

In Mérida, Capital of Yucatán

you can buy one cigarette, one needle, and a shrimp
curled up in sauce. In the lush
lime and mango undergrowth you can lie
in the lap of the god Chac Mool. In Mérida
you're no broke fool for sizing up
an onion in the marketplace.
You'll share as long as you can

leave. You're tired of buying
Chiclets from little girls
who are too bored, too small to be
an abstraction. These rancid buds
think you have something for them.
Shoeshine men on knees paint men's loafers,
avoiding socks, and shoo the girls away.
Niñas land on the next table of men
who snap the news from page to page. You drink

a glass of tap water *horchata,* fortify yourself
for the long way home, think the body can accommodate
bad water as long as its thoughts are pure.
Life gets longer. You're tired of talk
and longing. You want to go home.
In Mérida no clicks negate the blanks.
A cupped hand finds, fits perfectly
'round empty in the total dark.

Fullness

What is there to want?
All the work is done.
Girlclock, catclock, sunclock
tick in sync today.
Love/life, love/life, love/life, they say.

The world again opens
to wake us up in black and white
and lift the day to robin's egg.
We know our exact balance,
we have everything.

Trading perfume over garden walls,
wisteria opens for bee season:
men become handsome to the wives of other men
and women breathe in their own beautiful beauty.

The genius baby licks pollen from a gardenia
her father holds out for the pretty neighbor.
All give in to deliciousness.
What is there to want?
All the work is done.

And then the visiting on sea-blue porches.
All have something to show for the day.
The mail carrier strolls back to talk
about art for the new fire station.

As dark washes water-blue down the street,
our comet swings by loaded with the dream
that hums the world alive:
All the work is done.

What is there to want?
We know our exact balance,
we have everything.

Equipoise

I could build a wild bonfire
above the sea to get you
to notice me, but
I like the nearness
to an everywhere of light.
I'm not hiding; this
is where I work, I live:
a lightning whelk, room
on top of room,
spired to the top.

I like the little
implements of ritual,
how separate prisms
polished in the morning
gather a hive of light
at dusk and fling it
at the white fold of horizon.

This is no tower of myth.
I can't wear old clothes
of lonely keepers,
who dipped the last
cup of sunset
to keep the lamps alive.

We all live in fear
of shoreless feelings,
but inside
this giant spark plug
as sumptuous as grace,
I see freshwater

freighters and saltwater
freighters floating
loads toward home.

NOTES

The title "Lilies Showering Down" is appropriated from line 142 of Andrew Marvell's poem "Upon Appleton House."

The title "Betwixt the Flames and Waves" is appropriated from line 7, section 6, of Andrew Marvell's poem "The Unfortunate Lover."

The title "Until the Day Breathes and the Shadows Flee" is from "The Song of Solomon," 2:17.

The title "New Worlds to Buy" is taken from line 60 of Marvell's poem "A Dialogue, between the Resolved Soul and Created Pleasure."

The line "amphibium of stuff and death," in "Objects of Desire," is a variation on line 40 of Marvell's poem "The Unfortunate Lover": "The amphibium of life and death."

The title "While the Sea Laughed Itself into a Foam" is line 122 of Marvell's poem "The Character of Holland."

The poem "Ocean with Whale" is for Debbie Luster.

The title "The Wanton Harmless Folds of Dreams" is a variation of line 633, section 80, of Marvell's poem "Upon Appleton House."

The poem "Interstices and Protuberances" is for Elizabeth Ervin.

The line "First was the world as one clay made" in "A Dialogue Between the Shepherdess and Mowers" is a variation on line one of Marvell's poem "Music Empire": "First was the world as one great cymbal made."

The title "Through the Dark Sod, as Education" is taken from the first line of Emily Dickinson's poem #392.

THE AUTHOR

Kathleen Halme's first book of poetry, *Every Substance Clothed,* winner of the 1995 University of Georgia Press Contemporary Poetry Series competition, was awarded the Balcones Poetry Prize. She completed her MFA in Creative Writing at the University of Michigan, where her work was awarded the Hopwood Creative Writing Award. Halme is a 1997–98 recipient of a National Endowment for the Arts Poetry Fellowship. She is associate professor of English at Western Washington University in Bellingham.

William Fridrich